WEEKDAY M

Michelle Poplawski

ISBN 978-1-0980-0065-3 (paperback)
ISBN 978-1-0980-0066-0 (digital)

Christian Faith Publishing, Inc.
832 Park Avenue
Meadville, PA 16335
www.christianfaithpublishing.com

Printed in the United States of America

Dedication

I can't believe I am right here, right now, sharing what is in my heart in the hopes of helping someone! I couldn't have done this without the support of all those who have crossed my path and my Higher Power, who held me up, walked with me and pushed me forward. In my journey, there have been many who joined my ride and I thank all of you, you made me who I am today.

I want to say a *very special thank you* to a few. To my mom, Tina, thank you for never giving up on me and always wanting what is best for me. To my Godmother Annette, thank you for always being a positive influence in my life. To my daughter, Kristy, thank you for loving and supporting me through my worst and best times and being my "ride and die" person. To my step-children, Jonathan, Nicole, and Jason, thank you for opening up your hearts way back when to let me in and helping me to become the best mom and person I could be. To my sponsor and friend, Regina, thank you for convincing me that I have a gift that needs to be shared.

This book is here because of all of you!

WEEK 1

Monday

Good morning! My heart can handle positive and negative emotions but not both at the same time. May I focus on the positive and be grateful that I am safe in my Higher Power's hands!

Tuesday

Good morning! All changes start from within.

Wednesday

Good morning! Remember that the people who cross your path are meant to do so. These people help us on our journey.

Thursday

Good morning! Keep looking up and walking forward!

Friday

Good morning! Change is a process; today is as good as any to start that process. God will help if I ask Him.

WEEK 2

Monday

Good morning! The sunshine in our lives comes from within, may you see it through the storms.

Tuesday

Good morning! We are very talented people, may we allow those talents to flourish. The world needs all of them!

Wednesday

Good morning! We are not perfect, but we have an opportunity to be the best we can be today; we have to do the footwork.

Thursday

Good morning! Step out of yourself, show someone they are important to you. Small steps make the difference.

Friday

Good morning! If I am okay with who I am today, imagine how I will feel as I get better, emotionally, mentally, and physically.

WEEK 3

Monday

Good morning! Change is a choice. Let me concentrate on the parts of me I can change and get busy.

Tuesday

Good morning! I am meant to participate in the moment in front of me; now I just need to do it. Live today!

Wednesday

Good morning! The help I will need today will only come if I open up and share what is bothering me. I can trust my friends in the program.

Thursday

Good morning! The pains and unhappiness in our lives have gotten us to a point where we need help. Ask for that help and life will get better!

Friday

Good morning! Humility, seeing my life as it is and working with it. Isn't that the same as perspective? May I see me as I am so I know where to start!

WEEK 4

Monday

Good morning! My new life is full of lots of questions, but how can I ever hear the answers if I don't take the time to listen?

Tuesday

Good morning! I am both positive and negative. I choose which I want to focus on; both require the same effort. How do I want to feel today?

Wednesday

Good morning! I am a result of my past experiences. With God's help, I see this as a blessing.

Thursday

Good morning! As my playground changes so must my choices. My Higher Power will help me make healthy ones.

Friday

Good morning! Everyone I meet is either necessary for my growth or I am necessary for theirs. Make the most of every encounter!

WEEK 5

Monday

Good morning! I may be fearful of the things I feel I can't do, but my Higher Power is with me. May I see past the fear to the things I can do and do them!

Tuesday

Good morning! May I remember that God is there through good and bad times. I NEVER need to feel like I am living life solo again!

Wednesday

Good morning! May I see that the journey I'm on is one of growth through experience. I need to continue and enjoy the ride.

Thursday

Good morning! The feelings we feel tell us we are alive and that we care.

Friday

Good morning! When I stopped drinking and using, my life started anew. I'm enjoying this new one!

WEEK 6

Monday

Good morning! When we are in the midst of an experience, we don't always see the benefit. Seeing the lesson or message sometimes takes time.

Tuesday

Good morning! I need to learn new ways to deal with old emotions. My friends in the program and my Higher Power will help me.

Wednesday

Good morning! There is strength in numbers. Me and my Higher Power make two and two means I am not alone.

Thursday

Good morning! May I trust God's way today!

Friday

Good morning! Tolerance and acceptance go hand in hand. May I practice this first by being tolerant and accepting of myself. I am a diamond with rough edges; in time the rough edges will be smoother.

WEEK 7

Monday

Good morning! Wisdom about what is right for me has to come from within. While I learn from other people, I still have to trust my gut instinct.

Tuesday

Good morning! Before the courage to do what I can do and the wisdom to know what I can't, I must have serenity; a clear, unclouded, and calm mind.

Wednesday

Good morning! I will only be as well as I allow myself to be today. Let me start the day with positive affirmations… I am good and loved.

Thursday

Good morning! My choices are just that, my choices. Blaming others for my bad choices is not a luxury I can afford. I have to take responsibility for my life. The choices are better if I make them after praying to my Higher Power.

Friday

Good morning! Through giving of myself, I help others. God help me to share who I really am today!

WEEK 8

Monday

Good morning! The past brings with it the lessons I have learned. That is the part of the past I must remember...the lesson.

Tuesday

Good morning! May I see that with God's help I can accept the good and bad in me and walk tall again.

Wednesday

Good morning! Just as my Higher Power is helping me, He is helping my friends in the program. I need to stay out of the way and let Him help.

Thursday

Good morning! May I see where I've been as necessary in my journey. May I see where I am going as a contrast to where I've been and be grateful.

Friday

Good morning! May I remember that each of us needs to measure up, but God decides what that measurement is, not me.

WEEK 9

Monday

Good morning! May I see even when things are rough, that there is a reason why I am here. I may not know what it is, but there is one.

Tuesday

Good morning! Honesty with others allows them to decide if they accept and like me. Shouldn't everyone have that choice: what they can accept and what they can't, who they like and who they don't?

Wednesday

Good morning! It doesn't matter who your Higher Power is, as long as it's not you. Once you find Him/Her, the emptiness starts to disappear. You are not alone!

Thursday

Good morning! Spiritual perfection is impossible, but spiritual progress is not. May I continue to move in the right direction and work on progress.

Friday

Good morning! Unspoken gratitude is like faith without works. In order to be effective, I must tell you I am grateful for all of you who have shared and crossed my path.

WEEK 10

Monday

Good morning! My life is a choreographed dance. It's beautiful when I learn the steps and feel the music.

Tuesday

Good morning! The blessing of recovery is that I can be different from who I was yesterday. There is magic in that.

Wednesday

Good morning! My values guide me in decisions on how to handle situations. I have to know me to be true to me.

Thursday

Good morning! I need to work at fulfilling my expectations for my life. That is not selfish, but necessary for my well-being.

Friday

Good morning! My perception of the world is up to me. I can see problems or I can see opportunities. Do I have enough faith to see challenges as opportunities for personal growth?

WEEK 11

Monday

Good morning! God, give me the strength to face the opportunities for growth that I encounter today.

Tuesday

Good morning! Before I can be loved, I have to love. I have to start by loving myself. Then and only then can I love anyone else at any level.

Wednesday

Good morning! Faith allows me to do what I need to do and leave the rest for others to do their part, knowing that things will work out. Fear makes me think I have to do it all. How tiring!

Thursday

Good morning! The past is behind us. Today is a new day; let me treat it that way. God, help me to leave the past where it belongs, take the lessons I learned from it, and make today the best it can be!

Friday

Good morning! Tomorrow is not promised, so why obsess over it? I must do the best I can today and if tomorrow comes, I will be in a good place to live it.

WEEK 12

Monday

Good morning! I pray that God takes care of the outcomes today, while I concentrate on doing the next right thing.

Tuesday

Good morning! Today I can choose among my many options and those choices will be good ones if I listen to my Higher Power and follow His lead.

Wednesday

Good morning! Criticism does not build someone up; it tears them down. Watch your motives.

Thursday

Good morning! God always puts me where I need to be to hear what I need to hear. Today I pray for the willingness to listen to the message.

Friday

Good morning! If I ask, God will help me through my challenges. I do not need to feel alone because I truly am not!

WEEK 13

Monday

Good morning! Now that I have found my Higher Power, I have someone to walk the path of life with. It is wonderful to have company just for the asking.

Tuesday

Good morning! When I sit and reflect on my past, I realize that it truly is a miracle that I am here. May I live this miraculous day to its fullest!

Wednesday

Good morning! God will only give me what I can handle today. My job is to make sure I handle it today.

Thursday

Good morning! May God help me distinguish between my fears and the gut feeling that I should trust.

Friday

Good morning! May I start recognizing the quiet, uneventful times of my life as the serenity I am looking for instead of feeling like something is missing.

WEEK 14

Monday

Good morning! Being in touch with myself allows me to fully appreciate my experiences.

Tuesday

Good morning! Let me be grateful to God and this program for the freedom I have today, freedom from despair, shallowness, emptiness, and loneliness to name a few.

Wednesday

Good morning! I am thankful for everyone who has crossed my path. My life is fuller and richer because of you!

Thursday

Good morning! Things that happen in my life may upset the balance I worked so hard for. When that happens, I can turn to God and people in the program to regain it.

Friday

Good morning! To be free, I need to be me. My inner voice tells me who I am but when was the last time I listened?

WEEK 15

Monday

Good morning! Even if I don't understand the now, I need to see it as part of the journey God has planned for me.

Tuesday

Good morning! Being positive takes practice. I can practice by praising others' assets today. When I concentrate on the good, the bad isn't as important.

Wednesday

Good morning! I must stick up for myself and be true to me. It is about where I end and someone else begins.

Thursday

Good morning! Success is not arriving at the destination; it is in the journey. May I see the growth in me as I move forward as a success.

Friday

Good morning! Every relationship and encounter holds a lesson. How quickly or slowly I learn the lesson is dependent on how willing I am to receive it

WEEK 16

Monday

Good morning! Because of where I've been, I need to learn how to love and be loved, to forgive and be forgiven. God puts the teachers in my path; I need to be the student.

Tuesday

Good morning! When praying for guidance, I need to clean my thoughts before I start. I need to make sure I am listening for God's solution, not asking Him to approve one of mine.

Wednesday

Good morning! The challenges and difficulties I face are opportunities for me to see God's confidence in me. He is only giving me what I can handle.

Thursday

Good morning! May I stop and think before I act. I will avoid a lot of pain.

Friday

Good morning! Feeling the pain of my past will start my healing process. May I see that I am not seeing that pain alone. God and the fellowship are with me.

WEEK 17

Monday

Good morning! When I let go, it doesn't mean I don't care, but rather that I care a lot. God needs to step in and He can't if I'm in the way.

Tuesday

Good morning! Prayer is an attitude not an event. It is the connection with a Higher Power. It is the way I gain acceptance!

Wednesday

Good morning! To love life is to appreciate each experience. To do this, I need to put love in all my actions.

Thursday

Good morning! Although we experience bumps in the road, life is not all suffering. May I see that the good outweighs the bad.

Friday

Good morning! Self-esteem means I love myself despite my faults. Why shouldn't I? God does.

WEEK 18

Monday

Good morning! Success is not what you have, but who you are inside. Isn't being the best I can be inside a success story?

Tuesday

Good morning! Keep looking up and He will help you move forward.

Wednesday

Good morning! The day in front of me can be dark and dismal or bright and promising. My attitude will determine how it turns out.

Thursday

Good morning! I am grateful for all the differences around me. Every difference is there by design and adds value to life.

Friday

Good morning! May I see the crises and challenges I face as the turning point for a better me. Then may I take that better me and help make a better world.

WEEK 19

Monday

Good morning! God is always there and ready to help; all I need to do is ask for guidance and listen to the answers He gives me through others.

Tuesday

Good morning! May I realize that I must find the balance between work and prayer. Anything is possible if I put prayer in my work and work in my prayer.

Wednesday

Good morning! Life is temporary, but what I do in it can live on forever.

Thursday

Good morning! Every ending brings a beginning. Both are important to my journey, let me be grateful for both.

Friday

Good morning! Happiness is the result of healthy living.

WEEK 20

Monday

Good morning! We are each given a new start when we awaken. I must remember to stay in today, to enjoy the miracle of the moment I am in.

Tuesday

Good morning! The fire of anger will prevent the light of the spirit from touching your life. Why would I want to live in the darkness that follows?

Wednesday

Good morning! Today's experiences may be tough, but I am not walking through them alone. My Higher Power is right beside me. Can I remember that?

Thursday

Good morning! God's direction comes during meditation. The message reaches my heart and when I need it, makes it into my mind.

Friday

Good morning! I need to look at what parts of me did not work and ask my Higher Power for guidance to find ones that do. Let me work on progress...

WEEK 21

Monday

Good morning! One day I will follow God's footsteps. But until then, may I continue to ask Him to walk with me.

Tuesday

Good morning! To focus on today, I will make a list of things to accomplish...today I need to keep it that simple.

Wednesday

Good morning! I have a good and a bad side. I pray that the good one comes out on time today.

Thursday

Good morning! As I grow, my values will change. I pray that my actions follow suit.

Friday

Good morning! Life unfolds and things happen when it is right for us. Let me be patient and not try to force a door open. It will open when I am ready to walk thru.

WEEK 22

Monday

Good morning! Today is a new day. I am grateful for it and all the people I will share it with!

Tuesday

Good morning! God knows what I need and want. He sees into my heart. May I trust in this as my life unfolds.

Wednesday

Good morning! Fears are necessary for growth. As I grow old, fears will melt away.

Thursday

Good morning! I must try to trust my inner voice. My inner voice will help me move in the right direction.

Friday

Good morning! There is nothing to fear. Today's events are necessary for my growth. May I remember that God is with me.

WEEK 23

Monday

Good morning! The future is mine for the taking, but first I must loosen by grasp on the past. I only have two hands, don't I?

Tuesday

Good morning! Greet each day with a smile and love; you will be amazed at how that day turns out.

Wednesday

Good morning! I am a bundle of assets and liabilities. Once I am aware and accept that fact, I can work with both. Then I am on the road to personal success.

Thursday

Good morning! Every person on earth is here for a reason; that includes me. May I trust that my life serves a purpose.

Friday

Good morning! Everything that happens, happens for a reason. It is what I do with what happens that matters.

WEEK 24

Monday

Good morning! Be the best you can be, but do it with honesty, love, and compassion.

Tuesday

Good morning! To get through the pain in my life, I must acknowledge it, take responsibility for my part, and let God take care of the rest.

Wednesday

Good morning! Failures are part of being human. I can laugh about it and move on. It's time to try something new.

Thursday

Good morning! My past was necessary to get me to where I am today, but it doesn't determine how today will turn out. My Higher Power and I will figure it out.

Friday

Good morning! Reacting to life means someone else's actions took control of my emotions. Isn't it time I take action and control of how I feel and act?

WEEK 25

Monday

Good morning! Prayer is an honest thought that I take to God.

Tuesday

Good morning! Faith and a positive attitude are needed before we start walking the road to success.

Wednesday

Good morning! The new life that awaits me seems to take its sweet time getting here. Let me be patient and learn to enjoy the journey.

Thursday

Good morning! I must set time aside to talk to my Higher Power; it is the answer to my spiritual growth.

Friday

Good morning! Life can throw some curve balls, to which I usually say, "Let the games begin." Today I need to be healthy and say, "Let the games go on without me."

WEEK 26

Monday

Good morning! The contribution I make to today is mine to make. God has blessed me with talents. Isn't it time I share them?

Tuesday

Good morning! What I receive from the program is meant for me, but it also needs to be passed on. Someone else needs the goodness, understanding, and love I can share.

Wednesday

Good morning! Real freedom means letting go of things out of my control. I can stop playing God!

Thursday

Good morning! Habits are formed by continuous practice of an action. What healthy action do you want to make a habit today? Are you willing to practice it?

Friday

Good morning! Today I have a right to be me but not at the expense of others. May I remember to check my motives by doing a 10th step and honestly reviewing my moments.

WEEK 27

Monday

Good morning! Throughout each day, I will be presented with choices—choices to act good or bad. May I choose good over evil and have no regrets.

Tuesday

Good morning! God's teachers come in many different forms. I must make sure I truly listen to those who share my path today in order to hear the lesson.

Wednesday

Good morning! The best way I can help someone is to choose to do the next right thing. It will benefit both of us.

Thursday

Good morning! My Higher Power will help me fill the emptiness I feel now that I have let go of the past. I need only ask.

Friday

Good morning! Although I may not understand all of what happens today, I can still enjoy it. So what is stopping me?

WEEK 28

Monday

Good morning! Everyone has a path to walk in life. I need to make sure to stay on my path and let my friends travel theirs.

Tuesday

Good morning! Just as I have defects, I have talents meant to share. God will help me develop my talents, just as he helps me change my defects.

Wednesday

Good morning! May God help me to be present for every moment of my journey. It is more important than the finish line.

Thursday

Good morning! It starts with being honest with myself and my Higher Power. He will help me be honest with others, then I will get the help I need to change.

Friday

Good morning! Next I must stop worrying about the actions of others. Isn't it me I need to change?

WEEK 29

Monday

Good morning! The new me is waiting to be developed. My ego wants the old me to stay. Which one will win?

Tuesday

Good morning! There is a lot of good in the world. Why do we often focus on the bad? May I ask God's help to see the blessings around me.

Wednesday

Good morning! The feelings I feel today tell me something important about who I am. Let me embrace the feelings and that person.

Thursday

Good morning! In order to be there for others, I must first be there for me. In order to love others, I must first love me.

Friday

Good morning! May I slow down and listen to that gut feeling today to know what the next right thing is.

WEEK 30

Monday

Good morning! Before I can be close to anyone, I must be intimate with me. Let me take time to look inside to see who I really am. My relationships need the real me.

Tuesday

Good morning! What I want is not always in God's plan. May I remain open-minded and patient; after all, what God wants for me may be a whole lot better.

Wednesday

Good morning! Pity has no place on the path of change and growth; it will keep one stuck. Let me put something else at the center of my days, something positive.

Thursday

Good morning! The feelings I am feeling at the moment tell me who I am right then. If I don't like that person, I need to change the thought driving that feeling.

Friday

Good morning! What comes from the heart, reaches the heart. What helps me the most is when someone shares what is in their heart. Shouldn't I do the same?

WEEK 31

Monday

Good morning! I am the only one I have control of—where I am, my thoughts, and my attitudes, not the other person's. If something is not right, maybe it's me.

Tuesday

Good morning! The people I surround myself with indicate how healthy I am.

Wednesday

Good morning! Life is a process, not an event. I don't have to get ready for it; I have to participate in it.

Thursday

Good morning! Each time I stumble and catch myself, I gain strength.

Friday

Good morning! My true success is based on how honest I am with myself. When I'm honest with me, I get what I need…that is true success.

WEEK 32

Monday

Good morning! I must find a way to love the person in the mirror. It is as simple as smiling back at her/him.

Tuesday

Good morning! I heard from a friend that if I need to talk, God's number won't give me a busy signal.

Wednesday

Good morning! The sunshine of my day will come from within. If my attitude is right, the day looks brighter.

Thursday

Good morning! Today I can decide whether I will exist or live. I spent a lot of years existing, isn't it time to live the life God wants for me?

Friday

Good morning! Each moment brings a blessing, something to be grateful for. I have to live the moment to see it, don't I?

WEEK 33

Monday

Good morning! When the world looks dark and cold, I am not turning to my Higher Power. If I was, I would feel the light and warmth of His protection.

Tuesday

Good morning! My past is heavy baggage, but do I really need to take it on today's journey? Maybe I need to let go and lighten the load.

Wednesday

Good morning! The HOW of the program can help me today. Let me be honest about what I am feeling, open to others' suggestions, and willing to face things a new way.

Thursday

Good morning! Each day may not be the best, but it could be worse. Realizing this makes me appreciate today, the day I am living.

Friday

Good morning! We all need to have our troubles heard, but we need to hear others' too. Those around me need to know that I'm here to help and it can start with an encouraging smile.

WEEK 34

Monday

Good morning! To live each moment, I must feel what I need to feel, do what I need to do, and pray that God helps me to get to the next.

Tuesday

Good morning! I can't change the moments I have already lived. If, in looking at the past, I don't like what I see, I can live today differently. God will help.

Wednesday

Good morning! When I focus on what's around the corner, I may miss the blessing in front of me right now; and what if right now is all I have?

Thursday

Good morning! When I think I am so different, I find myself feeling alone. It's my similarities that help me to connect, get help, and be of service. Don't I want to feel a part of instead of apart from?

Friday

Good morning! Feeling grateful for what I have or what someone does for me reminds me that I'm not entitled...with that comes the start of humility.

WEEK 35

Monday

Good morning! My role is important, otherwise why would I have a part in this play I call life?

Tuesday

Good morning! To find happiness, I need to stop reaching for it. When I am only concerned with my happiness, it will elude me. When I help others, out of love, it is amazing how good I feel.

Wednesday

Good morning! When I think of completing a big project or solving a big problem, I get overwhelmed. But when I look at each step to get to the end, miraculously I see how small and attainable each step is. God, help me work on each small thing until I get to the end.

Thursday

Good morning! Sometimes what I face feels like too much to handle. That's because I am looking at it from a restricted view. When I pray, the view gets bigger and I realize I am not alone. Then the challenge gets right-sized.

Friday

Good morning! I am the only one who can change me with help and willingness. Isn't that enough work for me today?

WEEK 36

Monday

Good morning! My attempts to live right should be used in all aspects of my life, especially the ones that no one sees. Who I am when no one is looking is the most important me.

Tuesday

Good morning! Today will be so much richer if I honestly share where I am with a friend. I will feel better and strengthen my connection to those around me. What can be better?

Wednesday

Good morning! It is easier to take action to move forward when I am grateful for where I am today. It may not be where I want to be, but is it better than where I was? Isn't that a wonderful thing?

Thursday

Good morning! When I feel inadequate and insecure, I am trying to live up to someone else's expectations. Shouldn't being who I am be good enough? God, help me to be grateful for being just who You made me to be!

Friday

Good morning! If nothing changes, nothing changes. But it starts by realizing I am unhappy and unsettled with the way things are.

WEEK 37

Monday

Good morning! Next I must honestly look at why I am unhappy and unsettled. If I can't see it, I can ask someone for help, my Higher Power is a good source.

Tuesday

Good morning! Change may not be easy, but the alternative is I will remain unhappy and unsettled. What have I got to lose?

Wednesday

Good morning! Although change is personal, I need only to accept the help of the people God put in my life to teach me how to do it. Am I ready to be happy and settled?

Thursday

Good morning! May God help me to bring what's in my heart out and do something about it.

Friday

Good morning! When I feel that people are not on the right path, I must remember to pray for peace and serenity for them. God's got them too!

WEEK 38

Monday

Good morning! I will look to my Higher Power for the calmness to sit still long enough to get the message I should hear today.

Tuesday

Good morning! It is the relationships I have and the things I do, not the objects I accumulate that matter. God, help me keep things in perspective.

Wednesday

Good morning! Whatever happens today, I must remember that I am not alone. Through good and bad, my Higher Power is with me.

Thursday

Good morning! May God help to bring down the wall I have built around myself and realize it is hindering me, not helping me, today.

Friday

Good morning! The opportunities that we face today are the ones we are ready for. God opened the door and He'll help us walk through it.

WEEK 39

Monday

Good morning! Through our worst fears, we will find strength. We need only remember we are not facing them alone.

Tuesday

Good morning! Life is what I make of it. I have something to offer today—the talents and assets God gave me. Don't I owe it to Him to share them?

Wednesday

Good morning! May I see my successes in little things: sobriety, a positive attitude, being there for a friend, and taking care of me. After all, aren't these big for me?

Thursday

Good morning! For years I built a wall around me for protection. What I got was loneliness. How can anyone decide if they like me if they never see the real me?

Friday

Good morning! When I want to try to control the world and people around me, I have no faith that God is present. He took care of me, won't He do the same for others?

WEEK 40

Monday

Good morning! My dreams need to be ones I have a part in. When I make responsible decisions and act accordingly, those dreams will get closer.

Tuesday

Good morning! My attitude determines whether the glass is half full or half empty today. Let me be happy for the things I do have instead of unhappy for the things I don't.

Wednesday

Good morning! My gut feeling is my inner guide. If I listen to it today, I have a better chance of acting right.

Thursday

Good morning! Faith, courage, and love can help me weather any storm. The fellowship can help me grow these assets.

Friday

Good morning! Through the daily storms, may I remember I am not alone; with God's help, I will make it through a stronger person.

WEEK 41

Monday

Good morning! A quiet mind is an open mind. When I stop the swirl of thoughts in my head, I have a chance to hear, truly hear, the suggestions of a friend.

Tuesday

Good morning! Awareness of my attitude is one thing; doing something to change it is another. If I want a different result, it starts with a different attitude.

Wednesday

Good morning! For years, I was the person others thought I was. My identity came from those around me. Today the people around me are helping me find who I really am.

Thursday

Good morning! Finding the real me starts with honesty. If I'm honest about how I feel, everyone knows where I stand. Then and only then, can we form a true friendship.

Friday

Good morning! Once I realize that my decisions are not giving me what I want out of life, I should be open to suggestions. Why, then, do I do the same and think I'll get different results?

WEEK 42

Monday

Good morning! Once I make the decision to try something different, I must do the work. This is scary, but my Higher Power will help me find the courage to try.

Tuesday

Good morning! The only decision that matters is whether I will do the next right thing. This starts with the basic decisions to not use, get some sleep, and eat.

Wednesday

Good morning! Once I am taking care of me, the other decisions I make have a chance to be healthy ones. Don't I deserve the chance?

Thursday

Good morning! It is not enough to think I can move forward. My feet have to follow my brain. The work involved is worth it. Besides, my Higher Power is with me!

Friday

Good morning! With a little effort, I can be what I was meant to be…let me use this second chance!

WEEK 43

Monday

Good morning! The strength and courage to walk down the new path that will give me another chance to live is mine for the asking. What am I waiting for?

Tuesday

Good morning! In order to see the beauty in someone, I must take the time to get to know them. Our real beauty can be found in our hearts not on the surface.

Wednesday

Good morning! My fears of trying something new prevent me from finding out that I just may be great at it! May I continue to use the courage within to explore.

Thursday

Good morning! Although who I am is influenced by people and things around me, I am defined by my spirit who speaks to me from within.

Friday

Good morning! Let me see the beauty in what is in front of me at this moment. It is the only moment that counts!

WEEK 44

Monday

Good morning! I often try to avoid the emotion that I feel by busying my thoughts and actions with things. God help me to live the moment I am in to the fullest.

Tuesday

Good morning! Being the person I am capable of being is overwhelming. Let me focus on changing one thing I don't like right now. Don't I have to start somewhere?

Wednesday

Good morning! I am only a victim when I allow myself to be. I have choices and I am responsible for making the right ones for me.

Thursday

Good morning! Procrastination means I am at stop. Can I ever afford to stop and not grow?

Friday

Good morning! May you remember that you are surrounded by the strength and courage of those that love you.

WEEK 45

Monday

Good morning! I must find my true center, that part that makes me tick, before I can move forward. It is the real me that God wants me to take into tomorrow

Tuesday

Good morning! Life is full of "opportunities". How I handle them is where I see the progress. Let me ask for help before I react if my old ways jump out.

Wednesday

Good morning! What I do at this moment will prepare me for what is to come. When I stay prayed up, I am able to suit up and show up for life. How wonderful is that?

Thursday

Good morning! With the help of my Higher Power and the people He put in my life, I get to enjoy each moment. After all, He gave me everything I needed, didn't He?

Friday

Good morning! Keeping parts of me hidden, keeps the solution I'm looking for out of reach. To share all of me opens the door to becoming free from my problems, maybe that's what they mean by "we are as sick as our secrets"?

WEEK 46

Monday

Good morning! We all have a job to do… God needs us in His plan!

Tuesday

Good morning! We control what we do about what we feel. May what you do be a healthy action for you!

Wednesday

Good morning! Being in touch with the real me changes the way the world looks. Everything seems to look brighter once the angle and light are right.

Thursday

Good morning! I am only as strong as the roots I cultivate. These roots are the foundation I will build my life on. If I want a strong and fulfilling life, I guess I have to put work in the foundation, don't I?

Friday

Good morning! My life is full of so many blessings. Why, then, do I spend so much time thinking about what I don't have? God, help me appreciate everything You do for me!

WEEK 47

Monday

Good morning! I have a unique contribution to God's world, one that only the real me can share. Being honest about who I really am is the only way I can give what I'm meant to give.

Tuesday

Good morning! Today may be the beginning or the end of the rest of your life! What do you want it to look like?

Wednesday

Good morning! Today is another day to practice what worked yesterday: pray, share where I'm at with someone who understands, and try to do the next right thing. Practice makes progress. Don't I want today to be progressively better than the days I left behind?

Thursday

Good morning! When I feel "off", I need to take a look at my thoughts and actions. Are they honest? Are they aimed toward healthy living? What am I doing to remain healthy in mind, spirit, and body? What are my motives? Now...does anything need to change?

Friday

Good morning! I have a vision of what my life is supposed to be like if I do the things I should. Life doesn't always turn out like that vision, but things do change. Maybe that's God's way of showing me that it is His vision that counts?

WEEK 48

Monday

Good morning! Things may not work the way I want the first time I attempt something, but isn't there satisfaction in knowing I at least tried? Today I will feel good about the effort whether I make the goal or not.

Tuesday

Good morning! The word can't doesn't mean that I am unable. It means I don't want to put in the effort. When I realize it's the effort that makes me feel good and not the end result…maybe I'll do more trying!

Wednesday

Good morning! Once I survive the troubles of my past, I have a choice. I can choose to exist and let those troubles return or I can choose to live and make decisions to make sure they stay in the past.

Thursday

Good morning! With an open mind and heart, I ask God to join me on my journey today. Amen!

Friday

Good morning! In order to have different I have to do different. It's not as hard as it seems… God put people around me to help. I just need to open my eyes and look in the right direction.

WEEK 49

Monday

Good morning! We all have a story to tell. Sharing that story is important but so is listening to another's. It is in listening as much as sharing, that I connect to another human being. Life is a give and take.

Tuesday

Good morning! My past may be behind me, but the lessons from what happened and what I did about it is something I can bring forward. How else can I learn to have a better today? Isn't that why God allows me to remember? Today I embrace the lesson!

Wednesday

Good morning! Some habits just need to be changed and that's scary…to change something that feels so much a part of me. I need to remember that at one time all habits were new. I created those habits by repeating certain behaviors; I can change them by doing something different. Just try it for 21 days!

Thursday

Good morning! When I live in fear, what I'm afraid of becomes bigger than everything, including my Higher Power. But why do I give something that holds me back and hurts me more power than someone who can help me?

Friday

Good morning! Life is so much easier when I trust that my Higher Power will take care of the things I can't control… I know this, so why do I keep trying to do His job? Isn't mine enough?

WEEK 50

Monday

Good morning! Sometimes the blessings I receive baffle me. I wonder what I did to deserve this. But God knows what is in my heart and gives me what He feels I need to be a better person. All He asks is that I help someone do the same. Accept the blessings!

Tuesday

Good morning! A peaceful and serene life is built and takes some work. I must pray, do the next right thing, and pay attention to who I surround myself with. Once I put in the work, I'll be amazed at what I'll do to keep it.

Wednesday

Good morning! The paths in front of me have something to offer me. The one most traveled may be comfortable, but may give me what I always got. The one with no footprints may challenge me but may require change. What is the right path for me today?

Thursday

Good morning! Today if I feel empty; it may be because I'm looking outside to complete me. Unfortunately when I do that, when whatever I used to fill it (money, power, a partner, etc.) is gone, the emptiness returns. Maybe I should look at being complete by myself first… I can't leave me, can I?

Friday

Good morning! Making the decision to make some changes is an important first step, but it can't stop there. Those changes only happen if we take action. Don't know what action to take? Ask for help.

WEEK 51

Monday

Good morning! To grow up emotionally, I have to first take a look at how I handled my past and why I did it that way. Then and only then can I explore new ways to handle the present. No need to fear, God will help me if I ask!

Tuesday

Good morning! Everyone has a vice; something they do to make them feel good. When we do it to excess, we prevent the good within from coming out, but the feeling from within is the one that lasts. Why would I choose the other?

Wednesday

Good morning! Real conversations touch the heart because both parties listen and speak from their own. Doesn't that make our connections worthwhile and enrich our lives?

Thursday

Good morning! There may be things in this life that I don't like, but that's okay, there is a lot that I do. I can choose to let the things I don't control my thoughts and ruin my day. Or I can use the things I like to push me into action for a better day!

Friday

Good morning! If I'm feeling lost, it is usually because I lost a connection with my Higher Power, the people around me, or the beauty of life. When I sit back, I realize none of it moved, I did. Maybe I need to turn around?

WEEK 52

Monday

Good morning! Fear, "false evidence affecting reality", keeps us from seeing things as they are. To overcome it, I only need to trust that God loves me and will not leave me alone.

Tuesday

Good morning! What am I really living for? It is to reach certain goal—attain a certain status? Or is it the journey, no matter where I end up? I get to choose what's more important, the end or the ride.

Wednesday

Good morning! Before I could appreciate the help that God always sends, I had to do everything I was able to do for me. I used the strength He gave me and was amazed at what I could do. When I felt I could go no further, He sent me someone to grab my hand and help me keep walking.

Thursday

Good morning! If I always look back to see where I've been or worry about what is yet to come, I risk missing today. Isn't that the only one that counts?

Friday

Good morning! The changes in my life will happen as long as I move in the direction as my Higher Power. May the new year bring you blessings.

ABOUT THE AUTHOR

Michelle Poplawski was born and raised in the inner city of Chicago, Illinois. She was always surrounded by a diverse group of people and was sometimes considered the minority in the neighborhoods where she grew up and lived; moving from the city to the suburbs in her late twenties. She went to a Catholic grammar school and a public high school where she got good grades and used a façade to hide her shyness. She started college out of high school but didn't finish until later in life.

Throughout Michelle's life, loss and struggle were no strangers. Having to deal with losing a sister, dad, grandparents, a significant other, and a stepson along with having a premature baby, all before the age of thirty-seven, made life very real for her. Along with the struggles came pain, an emotional and physical bottom, and the success of making it through. With the struggles came unhealthy coping skills and the road to find healthy ones.

Michelle rode the roller coaster of life: from an insecure child, to a hard-headed teenager and young adult, to a scared mom, to a grateful human being and productive member of society. She existed and now lives life. She loves to help people beat the odds.

CPSIA information can be obtained
at www.ICGtesting.com
Printed in the USA
LVHW111445020822
725010LV00016B/118

9 781098 000653